By the Grace of God

*A tribute to God and my search
for my long lost sisters*

NORMA SHIFFLETT

ISBN 978-0-57872-401-0 (paperback)

Second edition

Printed in the United States of America

This is Norma Shifflett's Story

I dedicate this book to our Heavenly Father and Jesus. This book would not have been possible if it wasn't for them and opening up the door and putting the right people in my path to help me. God and Jesus are the writers of this book. I am their instrument. I want to shout to this world how truly *amazing* and *wonderful* they are and I want to share with the world our story and all the blessings and favors that have been bestowed upon me. And it's by the grace of God I'm here. I am forever grateful and thankful. God and Jesus are *awesome*!

I also want to reach out to as many children as I can that do not have a home and are being abused. If I can reach out to one, it's worth it to me. I would tell them *do not* give up.

God and Jesus are with us; they see us through the storms and they always turn bad into good and that they have a great plan for us all. We are all here for a reason. We are *all* loved by them.

This book is dedicated to my adoptive family and my sisters Brenda and Diana. I also want to thank my sister Diana for helping me type since I don't type and for her input. I would like to thank my cousin Mary for helping with the book by gathering pictures.

Thanks to my family and friends who believed in me to be able to write this book and gave me encouragement.

I would also like to thank Elaine for helping me with the computer and Christian Faith Publishing for publishing my book. I would also like to thank Paula and Marie for their helpful advice.

CHAPTER 1

My Earlier Years

It was another dark day in our house, of being abused, me and my two younger sisters. Our mom would drink, beat us and lock us in the closet all the time. My stepfather (which was my sister's father) also drank and abused us on a regular basis. Our grandfather also drank and would beat me all the time just because I have cerebral palsy. I have a mild case of CP, tight heel cords to be exact which would cause me to walk on my toes. Even though I had to wear braces night and day, God truly blessed me that my CP wasn't a lot worse.

Of course with all the abuse it left us feeling unloved and unwanted. I remember our mom cared more about her boyfriends than she did us. One of the times we were left alone to fend for ourselves, I remember one of my sisters got sick. I tried to do the best I could to take care of her but what could I do? I was a baby myself.

This was also very strange about our mom, she ate coal, yes coal, you read this right. She actually liked the taste and craved it. A neighbor came over one day and saw me eating coal, I had it all over my mouth. The neighbor asked my mom, "Why is she eating coal?" and my mom told her, "because she likes it." Of course that wasn't the case, I was starving. The neighbor took the coal from me and felt so sorry for me and my sisters. Our great aunt ended up reporting her, so my sisters and I were taken away from that household. Our mom tossed us in the car like she couldn't wait to get rid of us. It was the best thing that could have happened to us. Our mom had been given a certain amount of time to get herself together to get us back but she didn't bother. I thank the dear Lord for getting us out of that house, we are alive today because of him. I also am thankful to my great aunt for reporting them. I was four and my two sisters were three and one when we were taken away. It was indeed a blessing!

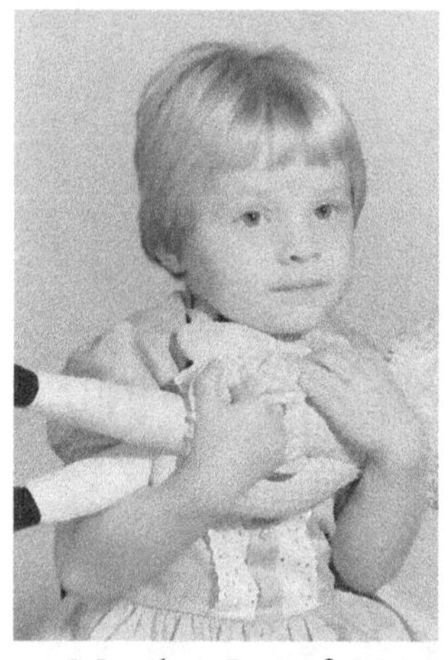

Me when I was four

After we were taken away from our mom, we went to live with Mennonites. They were three sisters and they were wonderful. I lived with them for a month but my sisters lived with them for two years. I would go and visit them on the holidays. After they left the Mennonites' house they went to live in a Baptist home for two or three days and then they were adopted into the same family.

Me when I was in the home for crippled and abused children

I on the other hand was sent to a home for crippled and abused children. I lived there for two years. It was not a good place, it was taking me out of an abusive home just to put me in another. I lived with two deaconesses. One was strict but the other, who was a teacher, was very abusive. I remember one day in class she asked me to read, so I tried and she said "You can do better than that!" and then she got a hold of my earlobe and yanked me all over the classroom. It was hard for me to maneuver since I had leg braces on. I was so embarrassed and felt so humiliated. The place had a boy's hall and a girl's hall. To me it seemed more like a hospital in that particular part of the place than anything else. One child's mother repeatedly sat her on the eye of the stove and burned her bottom. Her bottom literally looked like the hide of an elephant. I felt so bad for her it was so sad and awful at the same time that her mom had done it to her.

After I left the home for crippled and abused children (yet another blessing) I went to another foster home and lived with a family in Maryland. The woman there wanted to adopt me because I reminded her of her son that had died. I'm so thankful that her husband talked her out of it because it wouldn't have been fair to her or me, I couldn't have been her son.

I went to yet another foster home and they were wonderful. They lived near the Mennonites where I lived before. The man loved to watch *The Lawrence Welk Show* every week and I remember watching it with him while combing his red hair. I also remember falling off their porch and I have a scar under my chin because of it. I loved them and considered them my mom and dad. They wanted to adopt me and they were told if this other woman who also lives in Virginia doesn't adopt me, than they could have me, but she did end up adopting me, so apparently it wasn't meant to be.

My New Family

Finally a permanent home! I wouldn't have to move from home to home anymore! It was very hard when you would get attached to a family and would have to move on.

Miss Margaret Parker, my mom who adopted me

I was eight years old when Ms. Margaret Parker adopted me and she wasn't young when she did. In the court room the day of my adoption, after everything was said and done, my biological mom said, "Take her, I don't want her." After she said that, my new mom was furious. Of course, it hurt for it to have been said but rejection was certainly not a stranger to me and my sisters.

She was a wonderful mom; she was strict (firm but fair) and had a big heart. She always did for others and put others first before herself and boy was she fun, quite a character. She made birthdays, holidays and summers fun. Before she adopted me, she was in the Air Force for four years and she loved it but she gave it all up to adopt me; to me that says a lot. She was the first single woman in the State of Virginia to adopt. I remember her telling me that shortly after she adopted me, the first single man in Virginia adopted a little boy.

Not long after she adopted me, she adopted another girl; not blood related to me and she was six. Years later my adopted sister had a child, a boy named Ben and Mom ended up adopting him too. He was with us since four weeks old. My hat goes off to Mom adopting three children and never being married. It was crazy because first I was Ben's aunt and now I'm his sister, it's like the saying goes "I'm my own grandpa!"

Mom, was also a GS-12 in the government and she could never tell us what she did, so I would tease her and say she was a secret agent and laugh. I remember one day when she was getting up to get ready to go to work, she was half asleep and she was putting on deodorant (or what she thought was deodorant) but it was actually a bug spray! I thought it was so funny! We had a good laugh!

After she retired she decided to go back to work, she worked in school cafeteria's and she loved it.

We also lived with my mom's mom. She was also a wonderful person. She was very sweet and we were very close. I remember she would make Barbie clothes and take me for walks. At age eight, I only had to wear night braces, so it was easier now for me to walk and I was also going to physical therapy. I remember riding a bike, playing war and using the crabapples from a tree near our house for the weapons, and boy did they hurt! Years later, I tried ice skating and roller skating not that I would call what I was doing that but I had a good laugh. My mom said when she roller skated, she needed three skates, two for her feet and one for her bottom. I guess that would pertain to me too. The time I tried ice skating, I went with my church group and I fell and hurt myself. I had to be carried off the ice, which I didn't mind because the youth group leader who carried me off the ice was really good looking. It was worth it to me. Later he checked on me to see how I was doing, I told him I was alright and that my money that I had in my pocket had gotten all wet, so they were drying it for me in the office. We both laughed. Even though I have CP I wasn't going to let it stop me from doing things or at least trying.

Earlier, I was speaking of my grandmother. She was very special to me and I loved all the talks we would have. I remember her telling me she used to date Helen Keller's brother but she said he would never talk about his sister. I guess it's just the way it was back then. She also told me about one of her brothers that she was real close to. They were so close people thought that they were married because they were always together and she would just say no that he was her brother. She went on to say he was a fighter pilot and was shot down by the Red Baron and that his body was never found. My mom one day showed me a book that the Red Baron had written and she said that grandmother's brother, my great uncle, was mentioned in the book and that the Red Baron said that it was both a sad and victorious day because he had shot down Albert Griggs who he said was a very good pilot. I'm really upset because I can't find the book but I would love to have the book; it would mean so much to me.

My grandmother, Mrs. Mary Griggs Parker

My great uncle Albert Griggs,
who was shot down by the Red Baron

When it got to the point that we had to have someone care for grandmother, the woman we had was wonderful. When we would come home, we could always tell when the caregiver would say "*Well Granny*" that she had a good day, but when she would say "*Ms. Parker*", we knew she didn't have a good day with grandmother. We thought it was funny that it was a sure tail sign.

Then the time came that my grandmother went to live in a nursing home where one of my aunts worked. My mom and her other sister just always called her sister so that's why everybody else did too. Anyway, one day grandmother was trying very hard to tell my mom, my Aunt Sister and my Aunt Susan something and my grandmother was anxious. They kept trying to figure it out and then finally they asked, "Are you saying Albert"? As soon as they said his name, grandmother calmed down and it wasn't long after that that my grandmother died. We all felt that her brother Albert was telling her it was time for her to come home. Her death was very hard on me.

Mom and Me

Mom and grandmother would often tell me funny stories that I did as a child or other stories about other people that were funny. I have enjoyed sharing them with people over the years, so I thought I'd share some with you. When I first came to this family (as I said I was eight) my mom told me we were in church one day and mom was singing and I tugged on her skirt and looked up at her and asked "What are you singing?" and my mom whispered "Alto" and then not long after she answered me I tugged on her skirt again and said "Aren't you embarrassed?" Mom wasn't but she knew who was. Another time she took me to her Christmas party at work. When we got there, Mom was talking to some people and I ran ahead (as children often do) and was across the room and pointed up to this big picture on the wall and I hollered, "Hey, Mom! Is this the one you said looked like an idiot?" It was a picture of her boss! Mom about died. I'm sure she just wanted to disappear. My first Thanksgiving with the family, my mom told me we were all sitting at the table and I started talking about the turkey. I whispered to mom "They had to kill it didn't they?" and my mom was like "Not now, Norma", but I kept on and asked mom, "What happened to its face?" Doesn't he miss his mom and dad?" My mom was like "Norma, please hush". She was so afraid I was going to ruin everybody's appetite, luckily I didn't and I finally stopped talking about the turkey to my mom's relief. Another story she told me (which was true) is this couple was very upset because their child would always act up in church, and they asked people what can they do. The people suggested to give him paper and crayons and let him color, so they did but their child still acted up. By this time the father had had it. He picked up his child, put him over his shoulder and while he was marching out of the church, the little boy called back to the minister *"Pray for me!" "Pray for me!"* because he knew he was in trouble and needed the prayers.

I also remember when I was in elementary school, one of my teachers said to the class, "Today I'm going to walk different ways and I want you to tell me if I'm walking the right way." The first way he walked he was slumped over and he asked the class, "Is that the right way to walk?" and we all said no. The next time he walked he walked like I did on his toes and again he asked "Is this the right way to walk?" and again everybody said no and laughed. I was so hurt, humiliated and embarrassed; I just burst into tears. When it was time to go home, I went home crying and my mom asked me what was wrong. I told her and of course she was furious. She went right up to the school and confronted my teacher and asked him "Did you or did you not walk like my daughter does and humiliate her in front of everybody that all the children were laughing and it made Norma cry?" He first hemmed and hawed and then she asked him again and then he admitted it. Needless to say she let him have it. She ended up having him fired from the school system.

When I was ten we moved into a house that I loved and still do. It's the only stable home I've had since we lived there the longest than any other place that we lived (not that I didn't like our other homes). Anyway, the very day we moved in, another family was taken out of their home. The whole family was wanted by the law for a long time, even the mother. All of them robbed banks, hijacked airplanes and used their backyard for target practice. There was a lot of ivy and brush around their yard so you couldn't see in their yard. The next person that bought the house, she found a gun in the attic. It just goes to show, you might think you know who you are living next to but you really don't.

When I was older my mom went on a trip to the Orient. I was so glad when she went because, as I said before, she never did anything for herself, it was always for others. She had a favorite radio station that she would always listen to and the radio announcers were well known and they said they were going to the Orient and whoever else wanted to come along, to come and join them, so that's what she did. She said she had a wonderful time. In Thailand, she saw the actual palace of the King of Siam, the true story *The King and I*. She also saw the house he had built for the teacher. My mom said she also saw where the King was buried and that when she was there that they still talk about the King to this day. She told me about another place called Monkey Mountain where thousands and thousands of monkeys live and roam the mountain. The tour guide told everyone whatever you do, don't put your hands in your pockets because if you do they are going to think you have food. They were also told to keep an eye on their belongings because one time a monkey got into someone's bag and was waving someone's article of clothing (which was a bra not what you would want waved for everyone to see) back and forth, high above his head. My mom said a monkey grabbed ahold of one side of her purse, so they were pulling back and forth and my mom told the monkey, "Go away I don't have any food" but she said she couldn't get rid of him and wherever she went the monkey was right there with her. When they were struggling over her purse, Mom said it was raining and really pouring down hard. I would love to have seen that and gotten a video of it. I think it's hysterical. My mom said she also went to a place called a Thousand Steps. It was a thousand steps that you would walk up and then go into a cave. She said she actually made it up all the steps. When she was in the cave, Mom said someone else was in there (a stalactite, on the top of the cave broke off and actually took the person's arm off). It's awful, something you would never forget.

I remember a trip that the whole family went on. We went to California because one of my cousins was getting married. We all had a great time! One time in particular, me and my cousins were talking about mom and we were arguing about being with her in the same room. Mom was taking it as a compliment thinking that we were all wanting her company but that wasn't the case. We were arguing because none of us wanted to sleep in the same room with her because she snored <u>so loud.</u> The wedding was beautiful. When it came time to leave, I offered to go and find and get my little cousin and then meet the rest of our family at the car. Well, I found her drinking out of a spiked punch bowl. I went right over and got her and told her she wasn't supposed to drink that punch and that we had to leave and meet everybody at the car. All she said was how good the punch was, well I guess so! As we got in the car, there was another car parked in front of us and the car looked exactly like our car. I was thinking to myself that looks like our family in that car, sure enough it was! The car we got in was exactly like our family's car, so yes, I had us in the wrong one. I just told Mary we had to get out of that car because it wasn't ours and that our family was in the car in front of us. I felt like an idiot but it was funny.

I also attended the wedding of another cousin, who wrote a weekly TV show at the time. He married a well-known actress who was on a long running show. We had a blast. They were married in December and I remember Santa being in the street and we went to the reception on a double decker bus, which was a lot of fun, especially since there were a lot of celebrities riding with us. The actress my cousin married is a lovely person and very down to earth. She didn't let her fame go to her head, and she didn't act like she was better than anyone else. A beautiful person inside and out. At their reception, a woman who was drunk had crashed their wedding. She came over to our family table and sat down in my mom's chair where she was supposed to sit. My mom said to her that she was sitting in her seat and if she would get up because she would like to sit with her family. The woman said to my mom she could care less and she wasn't going to get up. Well, needless to say, she was removed from the chair and shown the door. She apparently was going around saying she knew the star (which she didn't and was causing other people problems). Despite the wedding crasher, the wedding was beautiful. The star's son was also there and it was his eighteenth birthday as well. My cousin and the star are not married anymore, they have been divorced for a long time. Last I heard, she got married to a lawyer and was very happy whether they're still married or not, I don't know. I would love to see all my cousins and everyone from that side of the family again since it's been so long.

My cousin Eric

My mom's sister, my Aunt Sister, who I was talking about earlier, was married and her husband George had a son named Eric. My cousin Eric and I and this other boy used to play Cowboys and Indians all the time and because I was the only girl, I would always be the one that was tied up and shot. I didn't care, we were all having fun. One night, Eric woke up in the middle of the night, not feeling well and Aunt Sister told him that she was going to call the doctor. She told him to go back to sleep and that she would check on him in a little bit; when she did she couldn't get him to wake up. Eric ended up having encephalitis (sleeping sickness). He was in a coma for eight years and then he died. They tried everything they could to bring him out of the coma. They brought his dog that he loved, no reaction. The only thing he would react to was when they would put the radio up to his ear; he would move a little bit to the music. I could never bring myself to go and see him knowing that he was in a vegetative state, it would have been too hard on me since we were so close. I wanted to remember him the way he was before he got sick. Eric was buried in his pajamas. The day he was buried, his father said, "When I die, I'll be buried in my pajamas too; if it's good enough for you, it's good enough for me". Uncle George was buried in his pajamas. He did that for the love of his son. It's so sad but at the same time you can't help but have it touch your heart.

When I was speaking earlier of Eric's dog, they used to have another one before that one and the one they had before was really mean. Aunt Sister told me one day she looked out her kitchen window and couldn't believe what she saw. She said all these dogs from the neighborhood had surrounded her house and was waiting for her dog to come out. Well, when it came time that he had to go out to do his business and she went to bring him back in, her dog was nowhere to be found. She never saw her dog again. What does that tell you?

My Aunt Sister

My Aunt Sister and I were very close too (actually our whole family was close) anyway, when Aunt Sister had gotten up in age, the nursing home where she used to work is where she ended up spending her last days. The people she used to work with took care of her. They were so good to my aunt and that I'm thankful for. My Aunt Sister was indeed a lady; she had a lot of class and she was fun! After she died she had wanted to be buried in certain clothing that she had specified and no one could find it. Everyone searched high and low and decided they would take up the search the next day, so when they went to the nursing home the following day members of the staff told my mom and Aunt Susan, "You aren't going to believe what you see when you go in your sister's room". In the front of the room, there was a table and on the table was the article of clothing that my aunt wanted to be buried in and right next to it a picture of her and nothing was on that table the day before! I miss and love my Aunt Sister, Uncle George and Eric very much.

Aunt Susan who knew the Roosevelt's, Eleanor and Franklin Cottage in Hyde Park in 1942 where she stayed while visiting the Roosevelt's.

My Aunt Susan was also a lot of fun, let's just say being mischievous runs in the family. We were all just a bunch of big kids. When Aunt Susan was little, she became friends with another girl in her school and her father ended up being President Franklin Roosevelt's right hand man. They got to be such good friends that my aunt was always over at the White House. One time she was there visiting,

Aunt Susan and her friend each got a cane of President Roosevelt's and a hat of his and started playing hockey using his hat for the puck. Roosevelt came in the room and my aunt and her friend stopped dead in their tracks (while thinking boy are we in trouble now) but Roosevelt said to them *Play* and they still didn't move and he again said *Play*, so they did just that! Another time my aunt was over visiting, Churchill was there and he was spending the night. His night clothes were neatly placed on the bed (Aunt Susan said he liked it that way). Anyway, his slippers were there and she and her friend each grabbed a slipper and ran but then they decided they had better put them back before they got in trouble, so they quickly tossed his slippers back in the room and kept running. Another story my aunt told me is that Mrs. Eleanor Roosevelt asked her what she would like to have for her birthday and my aunt said that she would love to have a pair of ice skates, so the day of her birthday Mrs. Roosevelt came to my aunt's school in the presidential limo and delivered the ice skates that she wanted. My grandmother went to pick up Aunt Susan one day at the White House and my grandmother had taken a cab and she told the cab driver to go ahead and drive up at the gate and the cab driver said, "Ma'am I can't do that, we will get shot at." Grandmother again said firmly, "Drive up to the gate", so he did reluctantly and when they got to the gate the guy at the gate said my grandmother's name and asked how she was doing, all to the cab driver's surprise. He went on to say "My wife is not going to believe this."

My Aunt Susan started to write a book on the times that she spent with the Roosevelt's and here is a little of what she started to write. *Mr. Roosevelt's right hand man and his daughter that I was friends with were playing dress up and had various large clothes which we made fit by bunching up the back and pinning with very large safety pins. Someone came to tell us the Queen wanted to see us and we found out that even in the USA, when the Queen summons, you are not expected to take time out to change clothes; we went as we were. My friend probably already knew but I had just previously been taught the proper courtesy for royalty (knee to floor). We were presented to the Queen, curtsied and the Queen chatted a little with us, then we were dismissed. We curtsied again and left, but I wasn't about to let the only Queen I was likely to meet see the pins down my back, so I did not turn around as I left the room. Later, Mrs. Roosevelt came to see us to find out exactly what happened because the Queen was quite impressed and told Mrs. Roosevelt that I was the only young American who knew how to leave the presence of royalty, I explained about the pins at which Mrs. Roosevelt smiled broadly, patted me on the leg, rose and turned to me and thanked me for being so thoughtful. From then on, in any gathering (dinner or tea) the Queen would suggest (through the lady-in-waiting) I sit beside her. Boy did I watch my manners!*

Aunt Susan used to be an x-ray technician and she ended up becoming friends with a well-known NFL football team because she was always x-raying their injuries. She would spend time with them sometimes, I thought that was kind of neat.

Aunt Susan adopted three children and she also married. He was my Uncle Ed. He used to be a police officer. Their children one of them was Mary, she used to come and visit in the summer and we would always do pranks on each other (along with the rest of my family). My house (a split foyer you can either go upstairs or down) anyway, I was going down the steps and when I got to the bottom, it was dark and I reached over to turn on the light and all of a sudden I heard the blow of a trumpet. Mary was waiting for me at the bottom of the stairs. I screamed and jumped sky high! We both had a good laugh! The next night I got her back, I put a fake snake in her bed. I know I'm bad. Anyway, she had gone to bed and I was waiting and listening outside the door for her reaction. I heard her turn the light back on and she apparently pulled the covers back because the next minute she screamed. I couldn't help but laugh! Another time I offered her candy or gum, I can't remember which Mary couldn't get something to drink fast enough. I purposely gave her hot candy or gum.

One time, I was over at my cousin's house visiting and it had snowed. In the back of their house, it was all concrete, it's where the cars were parked and there was a steep incline. When it snowed it became a sheet of ice and that is where we decided to sled. My cousin, another one of Aunt Susan's children, said to me, "You can borrow my sled and go down first." I thought that was pretty nice of him and I thanked him but I should have known that something was up when he was being so nice to me. Anyway, here I was going down this steep incline, pretty fast I might add, since it was ice. I couldn't steer the sled so I yelled to my cousin, "I can't steer this sled! How do I do it?" My cousin yelled back "Oh, I forgot to tell you the sled is broken!" I was like thanks a lot along with ready to kill him. Luckily I plowed into a big pile of snow. Another thing he would do is when he would come over to visit, he would always take off on my bike and him knowing that I wanted to ride it would continually whiz past me on my bike and wouldn't get off of it to let me ride. I still haven't forgiven him for either of those things to this day. We do have a good laugh about it now and then. Not too long ago, I sent him a card that had a picture of a bike on the front and it said *Enjoy the ride* and I wrote on it *"As long as it's not my bike"*! I thought he'd get a kick out of it, which he did.

Another time, I remember my cousin I was just speaking of and my cousin Mary and a couple others that went with us on a catamaran. It was Mary's and my first time (and last at least for me). Anyway, the water was getting a little rough, so my cousin told one of the other people that went with us to move over to the other side and I'm not meaning to be mean or anything, because now I'm not skinny myself but when she did, the whole side of the boat went straight up in the air! We were all scampering to stay on the boat (that catamaran tipped over too easily) We were tossed in the water and the loop of the rope had gotten my foot but thank goodness it was taken off my ankle. We got back on the catamaran and my cousin told me to lie down on my stomach and not move, so Mary and I just wanted to get off the boat. It was like a raft with a sail, not much to it. I did as my cousin said, lied on my stomach and the water continually hit me in the face and everybody laughed. It was pretty funny. Then my cousin took us back to land and Mary and I were so happy to be on land again! We all had so much fun together.

My Aunt Susan just recently died which was also very difficult for me and my Uncle Ed has been dead for a long time. Before my Aunt Susan died, God blessed her with being able to go back to Hyde

Park where she spent time with the Roosevelt's which she had wanted to do for a long time. It's something how God brings us full circle. When she was on the tour, she amazed everyone including the tour guide and said this is where he kept his canes and she kept commenting on other parts of the house of where this was or that was that the only way she would know is if she had been there. Since my Aunt Susan never got to finish her book about the time she spent with the Roosevelt's, I wanted to do it for her out of my love for her. I've been truly blessed for the family God has given me.

CHAPTER 3

The Search for My Sisters Begins

It was many years before I found my sisters but this is how I went about it. First I had determination and once I set my mind on something, that's it and I don't give up. I started looking for my sisters when I was nineteen. School friends remembered how I used to say one of these days I'm going to find my sisters. It was so important to me, since I remembered being with them when I was little. My mom always supported me in finding them, which meant a lot to me.

I first joined an organization that help you find your lost loved ones but that didn't work and they are no longer around. Years later I joined another organization to help me find my sisters and I worked with the vice president of their company and she was great! I gave her what little information that I had, their names and birth dates and after that they gave me a list of people with the same names and birth dates and I went from there. I did the leg work. I will add that with all the searching that I did all those years, there were people that tried to discourage me but I wasn't going to let that stop me. I was told where they had my records there was a fire and that my records were closed and that the only way they could give me any information is if my sisters were looking for me. I would also like to add that before I joined the second organization, I went to where I was born and went to the courthouse and ended up finding information on my natural mom but I was never looking for her or my natural dad. I found out what her maiden name was so I looked in the telephone book with people with the same name and started calling them all. One of the people that I called did end up being my great aunt and uncle. The great aunt that I mentioned in the first chapter that I told you my great aunt was the one that reported my mom. Anyway, I met them at the motel where I was staying. My natural mom was my great uncle's niece. I also met their son and he was telling me how he remembered my mom always eating coal and they didn't have anything good to say about her. They took me to where she lived (I wasn't going to but I did) and I will say that when she saw me she held my hand and cried. She had that long black hair that I remembered and she and me and my sisters are part Cherokee. I don't think I look part Cherokee but people have told me I have high cheekbones. It was around Thanksgiving that I saw her. I hadn't seen her for over thirty years. I couldn't believe what she said to me. I was thinking that she would have asked me "How have you been all these years?" "I'm sorry for what I put you through" but that wasn't the case. Are you ready for this? She actually said to me and I'm not kidding "You know Christmas is coming." In other words, she was saying "You can get me a present." She didn't stop there. She went on to say, "You know my birthday is in February." So in other words again she was saying "You can get me a present." I couldn't believe what I was hearing. I thought that was pretty gutsy. I was thinking *my sisters and I don't owe you anything, it's you that owe us.* So, after that first time seeing each other after all these years, I decided I would give her one more chance. I sent her what I thought was a beautiful vase of flowers and I hadn't heard back from her, so I called up and asked her if she had got the vase of flowers and she told me yes she had and she said to me, "I hope you don't mind but I gave it away." Again, I couldn't believe she had told me she did that. It ended up that everything I gave her she gave it away. Another time I went over to her house and had just walked in and instead of saying "Hi how are you?" she said to me, "You look like you have gained some weight." I'm like thinking *how nice, thanks a lot.* Also, when I was there at her house she was telling me that she had a boyfriend that was really good to her and he got a washing machine for her but that she was going to break up with him and I asked "Why would you do that if he is so good to you?" and she said "Well, because he has a patch over one eye, that's why." I thought that was awful and also while I was there she showed me pictures of my two sisters but she didn't have any of me, so I asked her why that was the case and she said she lost my pictures. It's funny how my pictures were the only ones that were lost. So, in other words my mom didn't want to have anything to do with anyone that had something wrong with them, her boyfriend that she broke up with because of the patch over his eye and me because I have cerebral palsy. I was an embarrassment to her. Needless to say I gave her a piece of my mind and then that was it for me. I haven't talked to her or seen her since. To me she hasn't changed since we were little, very selfish. Regardless of all that she said and did, I do forgive her but that doesn't mean I want to socialize with her and it hurts since I was the first born and not one picture of me.

The good thing that came out of all this was I found out from my natural mom that I had another sister that I hadn't known about. She was pregnant with her when my sisters and I were taken away from her. During our first meeting after all those years she told me about this sister and that she lived right next door to her! When my sister heard that I was next door, she ran in the house and then just suddenly stopped and we just stared at each other, embraced and cried. I'll **never** forget that moment. She said she knew about me. She said she, at one time, tried to find me. She saw this woman who had the same name as me but she said she knew right away when she saw her that it wasn't me. She said she knew about our other sisters too. We are half sisters. We have the same mother and my sisters have the same father. I'm the one with a different father.

My youngest sister Brenda with her children
from left to right
Little Lee, Samantha and Tiffany

The sister I didn't know about told me she never got away from the abuse. Our natural mom also beat her and told her "Don't tell anybody or you will be taken away as your sisters were." Her natural father abused her too. He got a hold of her wrist and burned it on the eye of the stove. He also tied her to a tree and would beat her. She has scars all over her body because of it. This is another example/nightmare of abuse that went on in that household. It's by the grace of God we are alive.

I found my natural grandmother too, such a sweet person. She told me how my grandfather beat me all the time just because I have CP. My natural grandmother is now dead but I'm thankful to the dear Lord I got to see her once again.

My sister, the one I was just speaking of that I didn't know about, told me about my natural father's sisters, my natural aunts. One of my aunts worked at the same place she did. I met her and we kept up for a while and then the last I heard she died. I met her sister also and we also kept up for a while and it's been a while that we have been in touch.

They did tell me that my natural father was dead. He had just died a couple of months before I found them. He apparently loved me very much. My aunts told me that he always carried a picture of me in his wallet and that he had a big picture of me over his bed and that he would always say "If it takes my life, I'm going to find Norma Jean." He wanted me but it was best that I didn't end up with him because he did have a drinking problem as did most of my natural family, which I think is very sad. He died of liver cirrhosis. My aunts said he was the kind of person that would give the shirt off his back. It makes me feel good though that he did love me and want me. Even though we didn't get to share life at all together, we did share the same birthday which I thought was something. My aunts also told me of a story they told my dad. She went on to say that somebody she knew had picked up a hitch hiker and that person had a bag so

Me and my natural dad

the person asked him what was in the bag. To the person's surprise, he answered "None of your damn business!" He was like "I can't believe he just said that." They had gone down the road a little ways and the person asked again because of curiosity "What was in the bag" and he again answered "None of your damn business!" Again, the person couldn't believe him saying that. Well, anyway, they got to the destination where he wanted to be dropped off and he got out and forgot his bag. My aunt waited a few minutes and my dad asked her, "So, what was in the bag?" and she said "None of your damn business!" So yes, it was a joke, my aunt got him good. She laughed but my dad didn't find it funny. I thought it was funny that he didn't find it funny. I myself have had more fun with that joke.

When I was finding out about my dad, I was told by my aunts that my dad never married my mom but that he did marry someone else and that they had two children together, so, yes, I found out I have yet two more half sisters I didn't know about! They are not related to my other half sisters. Finding out that I had three additional sisters I didn't even know that I had, you could have knocked me over with a feather! When I met these two sisters of mine, the first one I met, it was a nice visit and she let me get a picture with her and when I was leaving she said to me very nicely I'm not a people person. I can respect that some people do just like to stay to themselves. The last thing I want to do is push myself on anybody. If people want me in their life that's fine if they don't, that's okay too. The other sister when I met her and her family it was a nice visit and we would keep up with each other by phone or mail for a while, it would be off and on over the years but then again I don't want to push myself on anyone and I'm just thankful to have met my sisters and their family.

I did end up finding my stepfather. My first sister that I told you about that I didn't know existed, had wanted to know where he was and if he was dead or alive, since he was her father. I told her all that I found out and they had their meeting after all these years. I had no interest at all because of all that he had done but then I changed my mind thinking that it would give me closure. Needless to say, it was very awkward and I was so angry from all that he did to me and my sisters, I just let him have it. I will say this, he did own up to all that he did to me and my sisters and he did apologize, so I do appreciate that he did do that. To this day our natural mom hasn't owned up to anything and she blames everybody else. Like I said, I have forgiven my mom, my grandfather (who is now dead) and my stepfather.

CHAPTER 4

The Search for My Sisters Continues

What an experience this has been, along with the good and the bad. As I said in the previous chapter I joined an organization (which is not around anymore) and worked with the vice president. In order to help with the search, she connects you with talk shows. She had me go to a talk show in New York to make a plea for my sisters. I was taped before the show to put me on before or after there was a commercial because they don't put you on the show unless the person or persons you're looking for has been found. So here I was before the show and the cameraman was getting ready to tape me when he asked my husband who was standing to the right of me if he would please move over to the right a little more and I jokingly said "Yes please step aside for the star," as I waved him away with my hand.

They were ready to start taping the show and the woman I was sitting next to was looking for her brother and I do hope she found him. Anyway, the taping started so they tell you when to clap and out comes the talk show host, then all of a sudden the talk show host said *Cut! Cut! Cut!* and he was not happy. From what I understood, from what was being said the talk show host didn't like what someone had said in the audience and it made him so mad he kicked the person out of his studio, what was said I don't know.

They started to tape again, so we were again clapping. The talk show host walked out again, then we hear *Cut! Cut! Cut!* This time from what I heard, apparently a guy accidentally stepped on another guy's white tennis shoes so they had got into a fight in the back of the audience. A woman that worked for the talk show host had to sit between them for the rest of the show.

They started taping for the third time. We did the same, started clapping, talk show host walking out, then all of a sudden a guy that was sitting behind me stood up and said "I'm bored with this show" and I'm thinking *Well, leave.* I think he just wanted the attention and to be on TV. I didn't think they were ever going to get it taped.

When the show finally got started, one of the people who was on the show was looking for her father and she was saying he used to work for the circus and he was a clown. After she spoke of her father, they surprised her with her father walking out on stage. It was wonderful to see them being reunited. I was happy for all the people that were on the show that were also reunited with their loved ones. Even though I was happy for all of them, it was also very hard on me. I cried throughout the whole show and you know how the camera goes for emotion! I'm sure my husband was wanting to disappear under the seat and say "I don't know this woman, I'm not with her!"

After the show was over, I went to congratulate everybody and tell them how happy I was for them. All of a sudden from across the crowd the woman that worked for the talk show host, looked right at me and said "Your time is coming soon." Low and behold two or three months later I did find my sisters! I get a chill each time I tell this story.

Earlier I meant to mention that at one point during the show (and I thought this was funny) people that were sitting behind me all of a sudden started making fun of the show and one of the guys said to his friends, while pretending to cry "Please help me find my long lost dog named Sparky." I couldn't help but laugh (which I needed to since I'd been crying so much during the show). It's just the way he said it. Please know by all means I'm not making light of people that have lost their pets.

Anyway, the vice president of the organization hooked me up with another talk show. The talk show host, like the first one I went to, doesn't do it anymore but this one did host for a long time and is well-known. This time I didn't go to his show, I just sent a tape of a plea for my sisters to the studio and they put it on the air. Are you ready for this? It was around Easter when this happened. One of my sisters that I was looking for was getting Easter cards ready to send out. She got up from the table where she was writing and walked across the room and turned on the TV and right when she did, there I was making a plea for my sisters and holding up their pictures. My sister was stunned and just stared at the TV, the next minute she was jumping up and down saying "That's my sister! That's my sister!". She called up the talk show and told them I was her sister and guess what? They lost my number! She remembered that I had said in my plea where we were born, so she called up the radio station there and told them what had happened. They made an announcement on the radio (and I thought this was funny) and said "To the woman who just made a plea on the talk show looking for her sisters, well now they are looking for you!" The reason I say *they* is because the sister I've been talking about also called up our other sister and told her about my plea but she didn't see it because she was at work. Needless to say, I never heard the radio station's message but not long afterwards the talk show called me and told me they found my sisters! I couldn't believe what I was hearing. I had to ask them again to make sure I was hearing what I was hearing. I was so excited! I thanked them and ran all through the house screaming and out of the house telling everyone. Of course I thanked God and Jesus most of all.

Indeed a miracle! God and Jesus are awesome! There isn't anything they can't do!

We could have been reunited on the talk show but it would have taken awhile. It wouldn't have been right away and we couldn't wait any longer, it had already been over thirty years since we had seen each other. Me and my sister, who saw my plea on TV, reunited at a 7-Eleven in Richmond, Virginia. We didn't care, we met half way and we just wanted to see each other. We ran up to each other, hugged and cried, kept looking at each other, talked a little bit and cried and hugged some more. It was an exciting and wonderful moment!

Not long after that reunion, the sister I just reunited with met me at another location and there I met for the first time the other sister I'd been looking for, Diana. My two sisters didn't know it but I had our other sister Brenda (the one we didn't know about) to come and surprise them and meet them for the first time. Again, what a wonderful and happy time; of course a moment I'll never forget. By the grace of God and Jesus, we were finally together again!

Our reunion picture of my sisters
left to right
Brenda, Diana and me
Together at Last!

CHAPTER 5

The Here and Now

How wonderful it is to have all the pieces to the puzzle and not to have to go down the street anymore and wonder is this my sister or is that my sister? I'm so grateful to God and Jesus they have blessed me so with this miracle and have given me peace in this matter.

I keep in touch with my sisters Diana and Brenda. I am close to both of them. They are the best sisters ever! Diana and Brenda have talked over the years. The other sister we have we don't keep up with. My other two sisters (from my fathers' side) aren't related to Diana and Brenda, as I said in my earlier chapter. I don't keep up with one and the other it's been off and on but that's okay. I can live with that. I'm just thankful that I have a rela-tionship with Diana and Brenda. Over the years I've gone to visit Brenda and have always enjoyed our visits. Brenda has three children (now grown, with children) but it's great to be an aunt and a great aunt! I haven't got to spend as much time as I would like to have over the years with her children but I hope to get to see more of them. I'm very blessed! My sister Diana has two children. Her son Brant is now an adult. I'm so proud of him! He was just in a show (he mod-

My nephew Brant

eled) and there are some agencies that are interested in him and of course I only wish him all the best. Brant is also very talented with singing and playing the guitar (he taught himself to play) he can play the guitar behind his head and he also writes his own songs. Brant and I share the love of music. I myself have always loved to sing and dance. People have told me that I have a beautiful singing voice and that I'm good and that I should be a singer but I thought (and still do) that there are so many other people that are so much better than me. I just don't have the confidence in myself, plus the fact I'm a coward and a wuss when it comes to singing in front of a lot of people. I have stage fright. I was once in a talent show in school years ago and it was fun. I sang a fast song and people were moving to the music but I haven't been able to sing in front of a lot of people since. Brant is a lot braver than me when it comes to that. I would love for Brant and me to sing a song together and record a record. I think that would be a blast! Music has been a great outlet for me over the years, it helps me to forget about my troubles even if it's just for a short time. Needless to say, I lose myself in the music and music makes me happy and I will admit it has always been a dream of mine along with writing this book to become a singer.

I used to go dancing all the time at this particular place (it was my home away from home). I loved disco dancing and I used to do the spins and the turns. I would dance all night until the place closed and go home and dance some more. I would go from one side of the room to the other and I still do when I dance.

One night when I went dancing and I thought this was funny, I danced with my arm out a little bit and went around in a circle. As I was doing this, I ended up punching a guy I didn't know in his nose. The guy was standing there holding his nose and working it. I was hoping I didn't break his nose and I went over to him to apologize and at the same time trying not to laugh. So, when I went back to the guy I was dancing with to continue dancing, he said to me "Would you please give me warning before you go in a circle again, so I can be sure to duck!" I laughed and said I would warn him.

This is another incident that happened to me (but not when I was dancing) which I also thought was funny. I was at church and this guy that I knew asked me if I would like to sit in the balcony with him and I said "Sure." A little later he asked me if I wanted to leave a little earlier and I said okay. We were going down the winding staircase because that was the only way to get down and the whole church was quiet and the minister was standing behind the pulpit and he shouted "And the Lord Jesus said!" and right after he said that I slipped on the steps and said "Whoa!" I mean the timing and the Lord Jesus said whoa! I was hanging on the steps for dear life and if the guy I was with hadn't caught me I would have gotten hurt. So, after the service, my mom walked right over to me and said "You left church early, didn't you?" My mom knew it was me. I don't know what it is with me but things always seemed to happen to me.

My mom told me another church story about a boy who carries the incense pot but didn't have it with him. As the service started, the minister chanted to the boy *"Where is the incense pot?"* and the boy chanted back *"I threw it in the alley; it was too damn hot!"* And that was exactly what he did with it!

My niece Katie

Going back though, talking about my nieces and nephews, my sister Diana also has a daughter named Katie. She is a teenager and is really sweet and we are a lot alike in personality. We both speak our minds and say it like it is and we both have the same sense of humor.

Recently my sister Diana found this western town in Smithfield, NC that is not far from where she lives. Me, my husband, Diana, Brant and Katie went there and we all had a blast! We were greeted by the sheriff, Wild Bill (William Drake). He started telling us about his western town (it was so interesting listening to all he was saying). The western town is right behind his house. William Drake was an actor on the TV shows "Gunsmoke" and "Bonanza".

He was also in a movie with Clint Eastwood and he was the first one to be shot. It was the movie "Outlaw Josey Wales." He showed us the barber shop, the jail house, and yes, I had the sheriff lock my family up and me too. He was great. He played right along. After he locked me up I said, "I didn't do it. I am innocent!" while gripping the bars. After we got out of the clinker he showed us the chapel and that was my favorite. I always wanted to have a shotgun wedding; I think it would be fun but I tell everyone my husband would probably rather take the bullet and say, "Just go ahead and shoot me!"

Me when I became an outlaw, holding up Wild Bill (William Drake)
Do I look mean enough? :)

The Sheriff showed us the saloon next and was showing us the props he used in his shows. He was showing me a gun. I took it and held the sheriff up. Again he played right along and put his hands up and dropped a bill. He even went on to pretend to be scared by shaking real bad and acting terrified, which really added to it and I thought it was funny. Later, I burst through the saloon doors (which I was dying to do) and tried to look as mean and threatening as possible. I held up my family. I know I am a bad influence! I am sure you guessed by now I am a big kid! The sheriff made our time fun and memorable. I am ready to go back and get a group picture of us, all as outlaws.

My brother Ben

Another fun time I would like to share with you is when I went sledding with my husband and brother/nephew Ben who I spoke of at the beginning of the story. It was a great place to sled; there were a lot of hills in the front. My husband and I borrowed Ben's sled. So here we were going down the part that had a lot of hills. My husband was in the front and we literally went straight down and then airborne, straight down, airborne all the way down, what a blast! The second time we went down, I was in the front and it was a big area where we were sledding and leave it to me to find that one snowman and to run us right into it! We hit the snowman so hard I was tossed off the sled like a rag doll. The next time we went down my husband was in the front and we were going pretty fast, we were headed for the busy street below! So, I was like "Oh no!" I was just praying my husband would be able to stop us in time and thank the Lord he did. My brother Ben came down to where we were and told us that everybody was saying "They are going to go in the street! They are going to go in the street!" Guess what, my brother Ben told us that he was saying "My sled! My sled!" He could care less about us, he was just worried about his precious sled! I told him "I love you too Ben and that I felt the love!"

This was also funny I thought that Ben did (he's quite a character!) It was a long time ago, Ben was invited to a Halloween party and he decided to dress up as a woman. He called Mom across the house "Hey Mom, can I borrow your bra?" and Mom called back "No you can't borrow my bra!" I couldn't believe I was hearing this conversation. Anyway, Mom relented and let him borrow a bra, skirt, top and her red wig and red lipstick and he used tennis balls for up top. He looked like Annie. Needless to say he was the hit of the party! One of his friends came up to him and said "You are a little lopsided aren't you?" Years later we were talking about that party and he said (and I didn't know it back then) that the person that gave the party had a trampoline in his backyard, and he jumped on it. No wonder he was lopsided! I can just picture it. I thought it was hysterical! We both just sat there and laughed. You never would know what my family would do next.

One day my mom came home driving an old timey ambulance that she had just bought, (yes that's right!) and it was big. She painted on the back of it *Middle Age Madness*. We would go out in it all the time, it was fun. My grandmother loved riding around in it. I would always be in the very back acting like I was sick and dying and then I would collapse. Some would smile and get a kick out of it and others wouldn't but that's okay, we were having fun! Not long after my mom bought the ambulance, my Aunt Susan bought a hearse and drove around in that! One day my mom and I were out running errands and she saw this fire truck for sale and she would eye it every time we went by and I told her "Mom don't even think about it!"

I have another nephew and his family that I go and see. They just had their second baby, so, yet again I'm a great aunt! This nephew is Ben's half brother and he's a lot of fun too. Me, my husband and nephew went on a trip together and had a really good time. We went to the house where Humphrey Bogart and Lauren Becall got married. They were

My nephew James and his wife, Kristen

friends with an author, so it was his house where they got married. I enjoyed going on the tour of the house; I found it interesting. We also went to where Bob Evans and his wife used to live and next to that a big Bob Evans restaurant. I thought it was pretty neat. We went to some other places that I thought were pretty interesting too. Anyway, I had mentioned to my nephew how some people thought that I whined (imagine that!) and of course that's not the case. So at the end of our trip, we took my nephew back to his house. He immediately said to his wife. "My Aunt Norma *does* whine." He said I whined the whole trip, when for an example I at one time was saying how thirsty I was and hot. Again, not so. My nephew and I go back and forth about this all the time. I told him on my gravestone it's going to say "I do not whine!"

CHAPTER 6

The Final Chapter

Yet another blessing! Thanks to the dear Lord I found the Mennonites! They were still living where they had been for years in the same house where I had lived with them. They still take care of people in their home. They adopted a sweet girl who had a twin brother who died at birth and she herself has CP like me but hers is a lot worse. She can't walk, she crawls around everywhere and has the mind of a three year old. She is now thirty-eight years old. She is such a delight! She has a beautiful smile that lights up the room and she is always happy and she speaks a little. It's wonderful to go and visit with them.

They told me it was very hard for them after me and my sisters left their home. They would see me all the time because I lived in a house right near their house (the woman and her husband that I told you about earlier in my story who wanted to adopt me) Anyway, the Mennonites were told not to talk to me or anything when they would see me because they wanted me to bond with the other family. It was also difficult for them when they couldn't find anything out about my sisters.

The Mennonites also told me that when I left to go to the crippled and abused home (before I ended up with the couple that wanted to adopt me, but couldn't and were the Mennonite's neighbor's). The Mennonites said that their hearts sank when they found out I was going there because they knew it wasn't a good place and they said they knew people that used to work there but quit because it was so bad there. The Mennonites also said that my stepfather who beat us, used to come to their house to visit us but he was always drinking and in and out of jail, which I remembered was the case with him when I was little.

One day I hope to surprise the Mennonites with my sister, Diana, who they haven't seen since she was three. What a wonderful moment that would be! That would make the Mennonites so happy! I'm going to keep praying that it will happen someday.

People have often asked me what is the difference between the Mennonites and the Amish. The Mennonites are more modern than the Amish. They have electricity and drive cars and the Amish don't.

I also found the woman that wanted to adopt me! It was a wonderful reunion! But unfortunately I didn't get to see her husband because he had died.

Reunion with my foster parent, Mrs. Hoover

I also met other uncles and cousins I hadn't known about. They were coming out of the wood work!

I also found out that the home for the crippled and abused children was closed down.

My husband Gary and I. Our wedding picture

I married into a fun family (second marriage) and I have been instructed to mention and to put it in these exact words, so here it goes, I have a wonderful sister-in-law named Pam. One day I went over to my wonderful sister-in-law's house and before I got there I stopped off at a dollar store and bought fake parking tickets. I told my husband I'm going to have fun with these. I filled out the tickets (gag gifts are always fun) and my husband placed them on his family members' cars. They really looked real and it starts off saying this is not a real ticket but if it was I would give you two! My father-in-law had moved his car in the driveway and I had already filled out his ticket so it was placed on there anyway. So, he came out to his car and saw the ticket. He started fussing, saying "What? I got a ticket on my car? I'm in the driveway!" He continued his fussing and complaining and then my husband's nephew came out of the house and saw the ticket on my father-in-law's car and he joined in with the fussing and complaining. It took everything in me not to laugh. My father-in-law is one to fight tickets and he was ready to fight it! It was hysterical. Both of them stomped into the house, with ticket in hand. Me and my other sister-in-law were the only ones left outside so I told her "Maybe you should go check your car to make sure you don't have one." It took her a little while to come back from her car but when she did, boy was she mad. She came back stomping saying "This better be a joke because if it's not, I'll never come here again!" Again, it took everything in me not to laugh. Everybody else had gone inside, so I decided to but when I was about to go in the door, they had locked me out!. It didn't take long for my father-in law to figure out that I was the culprit! I knocked on the door and my sister-in-law said "Oh, you want to come in? So sorry." Then she closed the door in my face! I couldn't stop laughing. I was laughing so hard my stomach was hurting. I again knocked on the door and said to all of them that my husband should be out here with me because even though I filled out the tickets he was the one that placed them on the cars, so that made him my accomplice. But what was my husband doing he was in the house eating while I was locked out. Unfair, to say the least. It was pretty funny.

I was a preschool teacher for a long time and I loved it! I used to run after twelve two-year-olds and twelve three-year-olds. I adore children. I have done nothing else but work with children. I surprised myself by becoming a teacher, since the bad experiences that I had caused me to hate school but I think the reason I did was for one, the love I have for children; and two, I wanted to be just the opposite of those teacher's that were mean to me plus I said to myself I don't want to be anything like my natural mom and how she treated us. I wanted to be a good role model. I do hope and pray that I did make a good difference and that I have left them with good memories. I remember someone asked me one day what I did for a living. I told them I was a preschool teacher and that person said back to me "That's not any kind of job" Well, I grant you let that person be put in a room with that many children and I can rest assure they will be singing a different tune! I also had my own licensed day care in my home and I loved doing that too and I'm proud of that. I remember one child I had one day was upset because I had killed a bug that was scampering across the floor and he said to me "Miss Norma you shouldn't have done that" and I was thinking here we go and I said "But honey it was just a yucky bug" and he said (being very sad) "He was my friend." Let me tell you he let me have it up one side and down the other! You would have thought I should have given it a proper burial. I told him I was sorry and he asked me "And do you know what my friend's name was?" I said "No, what was his name?" and he said "Joshua". Wouldn't you know it, it was a name from the Bible, so I guess that made me a murderer.

I remember another little girl that was in my class when I worked in a school. I was putting on her coat and getting her ready to go home for the weekend. That following Monday we were told she died over the weekend. The other teachers and I were in shock. It hit us hard. Two people were racing and ended up hitting the back of the little girl's family's car. It's so sad. She was such a sweet little girl. We all went to her funeral and to see this tiny casket was heartbreaking. Not long after her death we got a new little girl in our class. We were all taken aback because this new little girl had the same name as the one that just died and she looked like her except the new child had different color hair.

I haven't been able to work for a very long time. There's been a lot of health issues. I have had cancer scares and organs removed. I might have to have another surgery too. There has been lots of doctors appointments, tests, surgeries over the years. At one time they were keeping an eye on me for breast cancer because I had a group of calcifications. I was told when there is a group of them, they keep a close watch, which they need to with me. When I found my family, I found out that a lot of my biological family has dropped dead like flies because of cancer. I also have nodules on my thyroid so I've had to have a needle aspiration and it's awful. I've had to have it more than once. They don't put you to sleep and they put these real long needles in your throat and move them around and you feel it. One time one of the needles hit something in my throat and I just burst into tears. Every time I would have to have this done at the hospital, I always felt like I was walking to my death as I was walking down the long hospital hall. It's anything but a picnic.

Back in 1991 I almost died. I had to have three operations within three months. It all started when I was having a lot of pain in my right arm. I kept thinking it would go away but it didn't. I went to the doctor and they were treating me for carpal tunnel syndrome since my fingertips were blue. So I went back for a follow up. The nurse was taking my vital signs and then she excused herself and brought the doctor. He examined me and said to me "I don't know what's going on with you but you don't have a pulse in your right wrist so I want you to go to the hospital now." It ended up that I was born with an extra rib and the rib was pressing down on an artery in my neck and that I had an aneurysm on the left side of my neck.

The reason my right arm was hurting so bad is because I had several blood clots in my arm and for that surgery they don't put you to sleep and I felt everything. The doctor was amazed how many blood clots I had. The first surgery they removed the extra rib on the one side and the aneurysm. The second surgery they removed the rib on the other side. It was that surgery that I was told I almost died, that they had to really work fast because I was literally bleeding to death. The third surgery was the blood clots being removed. It's indeed a miracle and a blessing that I am here. The doctor said I shouldn't even be here. I should be so many feet under. I've also been blessed by not having cancer all these years and God is so amazing he took away the calcifications too! I'm truly grateful! The most recent gift he has given me is this other surgery I thought I was going to have but is now put on hold and my surgeon is keeping an eye on me. Again, I'm so thankful! One of my doctors said that I have really been sick all my life, which is true but through it all I've been blessed in so many ways. I've told my doctors that I am tired of them and that I am allergic to them!

Most of my family who I was adopted into have gone home to the Lord. I miss and love them very much and I will treasure the good memories of all the fun times we had.

Right after my mom died, paranormal activity started happening (and it still does) To give a couple of examples, one day I was putting things on the closet shelf in our TV room and all of a sudden I felt her presence and you know how people have a certain scent like perfume. I knew it was my mom. Another time I was in the TV room reading and it had gotten real late, so I thought I really should get to bed. As I was climbing into the bed (and I kid you not) I felt a slap on my leg and I leaped across the bed and at the side where my husband was sleeping, at the end of the bed, (and again I kid you not) there was this big bright white mass! I was trying to wake up my husband but to no avail, he was out like a light. Anyway, I jumped in the covers and was cowardly scrunched under the covers. I looked over to where the bright white mass was and it was still there. It was there for a while. I closed my eyes and then when I opened them again the bright white mass was gone. I know it was my mom having a little fun with me, since she was mischievous. I told my husband about all that goes on and he doesn't believe in ghosts. I told him when I'm gone that I am going to come back and haunt him and make a believer out of him!

I did have a couple of angels visit me too. My unusual encounter that I had with the first angel (which was a long time ago) was when I went into a grocery store one day. I complimented the woman that was in the florist and told her how pretty the flower arrangements looked. She started talking to me about a situation that she and her daughter had been in that wasn't good but that God helped her. Now she and her daughter were happy and that God was her husband. Her situation she was telling me about that she had been in I could relate to. I went on to tell her I was glad to hear that everything was better for her and her daughter and that they were happy now. The next minute she looked right in my eyes and said to me very seriously "God is your husband, do you understand?" and I said "Yes." Then, I walked away and looked back to where she was and she was gone! I knew that was a message for me from God.

The second encounter with an angel, I was just walking down the sidewalk in a small shopping center, when all of a sudden I see this angel and I just stopped in my tracks and couldn't move, I was just so stunned. She just started talking to me and said "Your smile does brighten people's day and that I do shine." She went on to say "Jesus loves you", then she was gone. I had been saying every day to God "Please tell me that when I smile that I am able to lift a person's spirits and get them to smile and make their day a little brighter, and that I do shine." So I got my answer! I can't describe to you in detail what she looked like, because I was so shocked. Angels are here one minute and gone the next. I feel so honored and blessed to have been visited by them.

I'm so thankful and blessed to have my long lost sisters. It's really something all these years of being apart, we were not far from each other and didn't even know it. We only lived two or three hours from each other!

One of my friends just recently asked me if I had any repercussions from all that I've been through and I told her yes. For one thing, I had nightmares for years because of the abuse. My nightmares didn't stop until I was in my mid-forties. Also, I am claustrophobic for always being locked in the closet. Sometimes I also have a hard time understanding and comprehending when someone is trying to explain something to me, or if I am reading something. Even if the person tries to explain things to me again or I reread what I was reading sometimes, I still don't understand and I feel like an idiot but I know it's because of the coal that was given to me when I was little. I have also struggled with depression over the years because of the abuse but I'm doing so much better with that now. I just turn (what's too big for me) my worries and concerns over to God and Jesus. They always ease my worries and concerns and they are the *only* answer.

I'm hoping and praying that my sisters and I will all be able to be together again and to be sisters and do sisterly things. Since we have missed out on so much, I go and see each of them when I can (and I do treasure those times) but different circumstances have prevented us from being together as much as we would like, such as my illnesses, tests and surgeries. My sisters have their own busy lives, sometimes working two jobs and financial reasons. I am just going to keep the faith.

In closing, I would just like to say again, I hope I was able to give someone else hope and comfort that is out there that doesn't have a home and is being abused, that God does turn bad into good.

I would also like to end the story by saying:

- By the grace of God, my sisters and I are alive today.
- By the grace of God, I was adopted into a wonderful family.
- By the grace of God, I found my sister's.
- By the grace of God, I'm alive today...despite my illnesses.
- I will continue to say that he has healed me.

I hope I have succeeded in giving God and Jesus the praise and recognition that is so deserved. Again, this book has come together because of our Almighty God, who I will forever praise and be grateful too.

God Bless!

Addendum:

In July 2016, my stepfather died. At the end of October 2016, one of the Mennonite's died, and December 1, 2016, my adopted sister died.

Aunt Sister, Aunt Susan and Mom
doing their monkey faces

ABOUT THE AUTHOR

Norma Shifflett is a former preschool teacher from Virginia. She enjoys traveling, singing, watching movies, and dancing.